DELAWARE

Past and Present

Philip Wolny

rosen publishing's
rosen central®

New York

For Brandon Simpson

Published in 2010 by The Rosen Publishing Group, Inc.
29 East 21st Street, New York, NY 10010

Copyright © 2010 by The Rosen Publishing Group, Inc.

First Edition

Library of Congress Cataloging-in-Publication Data

Wolny, Philip.
Delaware: past and present / Philip Wolny.—1st ed.
    p. cm.—(The United States: past and present)
Includes bibliographical references and index.
ISBN 978-1-4358-3526-9 (library binding)
ISBN 978-1-4358-8502-8 (pbk)
ISBN 978-1-4358-8503-5 (6 pack)
1. Delaware—Juvenile literature. I. Title.
F164.3.W656 2010
975.1—dc22

                                                    2009024554

Manufactured in the United States of America

CPSIA Compliance Information: Batch #LW10YA: For Further Information contact Rosen Publishing, New York, New York at 1-800-237-9932

On the cover: Top left: Swedish colonists trade with Native Americans at New Sweden, in present-day Delaware. Top right: The Wilmington skyline. Bottom: People walk along the Riverfront in Wilmington, Delaware.

Contents

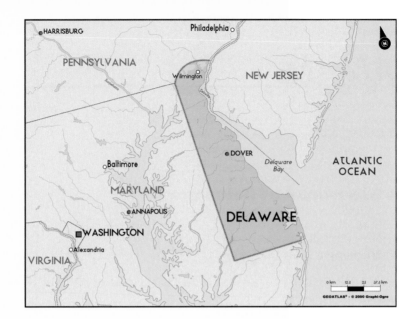

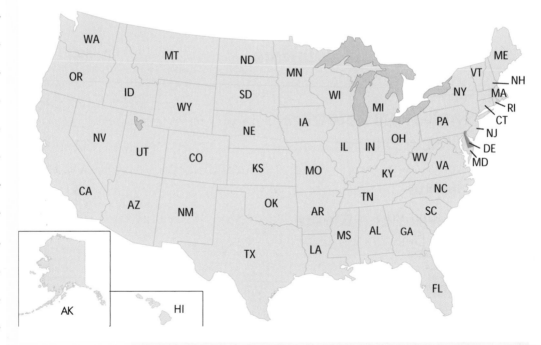

Delaware is located on the eastern seaboard of the United States. Its location is shown in relation to those of other states *(bottom)*, and also relative to its neighbors in the Mid-Atlantic region.

Introduction

In July 1776, the Continental Congress was busy in Philadelphia, Pennsylvania, ready to vote on whether the American colonies would declare independence from Britain. Each colony had one vote, determined by its individual delegates. But two of Delaware's three delegates, Thomas McKean and George Read, were deadlocked, with McKean voting for independence and Read against.

Caesar Rodney, the third delegate, had left earlier to deal with pro-British uprisings in Delaware's Sussex County. Urgent word was sent via messenger: he was needed immediately in Philadelphia.

An exhausted Rodney, suffering from cancer and asthma, appeared on Tuesday, July 2, after an 80-mile (129 kilometer) journey through thunderstorms over rough terrain. Though accounts vary whether he arrived on horseback or by carriage, he appeared just in time. He made the crucial vote, breaking the deadlock. Delaware would vote in favor of the Declaration of Independence.

Rodney's heroic ride is one of the better-known stories in the history of Delaware, a small state with a long and proud history. It has gone by many nicknames over the years. It is known as the Blue Hen state, after the blue hen chicken, the state bird. One of the Founding Fathers, Thomas Jefferson, declared it the Diamond State because of its strategic location. Due to its size, it has also been called Small Wonder.

Delaware was also the first of the original U.S. colonies to sign the Constitution on December 7, 1787. For this reason, in 2002, Delaware adopted a new official nickname: the First State.

In this book, we will examine Delaware's geography and history. We will show how its government works and how manufacturing, agriculture, services, and other activities drive its economy. We will also meet a few key individuals important to the state's history. In addition, we will examine snapshots of how the state has changed from earlier eras and how it has retained its essential spirit, typified by the brave, determined, and enduring Caesar Rodney.

Welcome to Delaware, past and present.

Chapter 1

THE GEOGRAPHY OF DELAWARE

Delaware is located on the eastern seaboard of the United States. Considered one of the Mid-Atlantic states, it lies on the Delmarva Peninsula. The Delmarva Peninsula gets its name from the fact that it is made up of Delaware, Maryland, and Virginia. Maryland lies to Delaware's south and west, and the small northern section of the First State borders Pennsylvania. Across the Delaware River and Delaware Bay lies New Jersey. Most of the state's western side is coastland facing Delaware Bay, with its southernmost coast running along the Atlantic Ocean.

The Coastal Plain and the Piedmont

Delaware has two distinct geographical regions. Most of the state is part of the Atlantic Coastal Plain, a region of the United States extending from New Jersey to Florida. In Delaware, this region is made up of flat plains at low elevations. Most of it rises no higher than 80 feet (24 meters) above sea level.

The state's other distinct land area makes up its northernmost section. This is known as the Piedmont. It is also part of a larger region that extends from New Jersey down to Alabama, forming a natural boundary between the Atlantic Coastal Plain and the

Marsh grass is plentiful in Bombay Hook National Wildlife Refuge. The refuge includes nearly 16,000 acres (6,475 hectares) on Delaware Bay in Kent County.

Appalachian Mountains. In Delaware, the Piedmont is characterized by rolling hills and fertile valleys. Delaware's highest point is in this region. It is located on Ebright Road in New Castle County, about 448 feet (137 m) above sea level. Delaware's mean, or average, elevation is 60 feet (18 m) above sea level, while most of its coastal areas are near or exactly at sea level.

According to the official state Web site (www.delaware.gov), Delaware's total area is only 1,982 square miles (5,133 square km). This makes it the second smallest state after Rhode Island, or forty-ninth in area in the nation. From east to west, its narrowest point is 9 miles (14 km) across, and its widest point is 35 miles (56 km) across. From north to south, Delaware is only 96 miles (154 km) long. Its coastline along the Atlantic is about 26 miles (42 km) long, while total shoreline, counting Delaware Bay, is about 260 miles (418 km).

Delaware's Counties

Delaware is divided into three counties from north to south: New Castle County, Kent County, and Sussex County. New Castle County, which includes the metropolitan area of Wilmington, is the northernmost and smallest county, and the most developed. Kent County lies in the center of the state and includes the state capital, Dover, and its surrounding areas. Sussex County, the largest of the three, lies in the south. Western Sussex County accounts for much of the state's agricultural output, while the eastern section includes its beaches and seaside resort areas.

An aerial view of Fort Delaware State Park and Chateau Country, both in New Castle County, provides one example of the state's pleasant landscapes.

PAST
AND
PRESENT

Delaware's Cypress Swamps and Trap Pond

Originally, much of Delaware was covered by forest. During the colonial era, if you visited southwestern Sussex County, near the town of Laurel, you would find yourself in a region of freshwater wetlands. This area was once known as the Delaware Everglades and consisted of 50,000 acres (20,234 hectares) of cypress swamp, with bald cypress trees that were centuries old.

According to Delaware's Forest Service, only about 30 percent of Delaware's land is now forested, mostly privately owned timberland. The sprawling cypress swamp of earlier years is mostly gone. Logging, agriculture, population growth, and development claimed much of it.

Today, smaller numbers of the trees remain. Along with the remaining swamp areas, they are preserved as Trap Pond State Park. The park also boasts a number of American holly trees, Delaware's official state tree. The pond for which the park is named was created in the late 1700s to power a sawmill that processed the area's harvested bald cypress trees. During the Great Depression, in order to create jobs and give people some recreational opportunities during hard times, the federal government bought Trap Pond and surrounding farmland. The Civilian Conservation Corps began to develop the area as parkland. Established in 1951, Trap Pond State Park became Delaware's first state park.

Nowadays, the park still serves as an idyllic getaway for nature lovers. Hiking trails surround the pond, and kayaks, pedal boats, rowboats, canoes, and small motor and fishing boats ply the waters. Sharp-eyed birdwatchers are likely to spot great blue herons, owls, hummingbirds, warblers, bald eagles, and pileated woodpeckers. The bald cypresses that still grow in the park are the northernmost stand of such trees on the East Coast and provide a small reminder of the natural scenery that once existed.

Weather and Climate

Delaware has a moderate, year-round climate. The mountains of Delaware's neighbor, Pennsylvania, help shield the state from cold air that streams in from the Northwest, resulting in mild winters. Similarly, the Atlantic Ocean keeps the summers warm, though quite humid, with some thunderstorm activity.

Delaware is typically coldest in January, with an average temperature of 35 degrees Fahrenheit (2 degrees Celsius). The hottest month is usually July, with an average temperature of 76°F (24°C). The south tends to have warmer winters, though summers are only a bit warmer there than in the north. When it comes to agriculture, Delaware's growing season varies between approximately 170 to 200 days out of the year.

Delaware's Waterways

Delaware has several short rivers that crisscross the state, most of them flowing east into Delaware Bay. These include the Mispillion, St. Jones, Leipsic, Broadkill, and Smyrna rivers. The Christina River and Brandywine Creek in northern Delaware are tributaries of the Delaware River.

Despite its name, the Delaware River borders only a small part of the northernmost section of the state. However, it drains into Delaware Bay and provides Wilmington, Delaware, with valuable shipping access to upriver destinations like Trenton (the capital of New Jersey) and Philadelphia.

Much of Delaware's coast lies on Delaware Bay, which is fed by the Delaware River and numerous smaller rivers and streams.

The lower Delaware River is visible here from the city of New Castle. The Delaware Memorial Bridge—actually two bridges that connect Delaware and New Jersey—is seen in the distance.

Farther south, its oceanfront includes a 26-mile (42 km) stretch of sandy beach, largely unbroken except for an inlet that opens into lagoons and bays. Mudflats and salt marshes make up much of the bay's shores.

Chapter 2

THE HISTORY OF DELAWARE

Delaware traces its beginnings to America's colonial era. Its original inhabitants were Native American tribes, primarily the Lenape people. The Lenape were hunters, farmers, and fishers living in what would become Delaware and neighboring areas. In the decades following European colonization of the "New World," they steadily lost their land to the newly arrived settlers from the "Old World."

Henry Hudson, an Englishman working for the Dutch East India Company, was perhaps the first European to explore the region in 1609. A year later, Captain Samuel Argall, an Englishman from the Virginia colony to the south, sailed into Delaware Bay. He named the area after Virginia's governor at the time, Thomas West, Lord De La Warr.

The Colonial Era

In 1631, Dutch settlers attempted to establish the first colony at Zwaanendael, now the town of Lewes. But they clashed with local Native American tribes, who destroyed their colony the following year. In 1638, Swedish settlers founded New Sweden at Fort Christina, the future site of Wilmington.

The Dutch still claimed the area, however, and later captured New Sweden, annexing it to their New Netherland colony in 1655.

William Penn accepts a belt from Tamanend, chief of the Lenni-Lenape Indians. This was part of a treaty to purchase land from the Indians, in Kensington, Delaware, in 1682.

New Netherland included parts of modern-day Delaware, New Jersey, Pennsylvania, New York, Connecticut, and Rhode Island. Finally, in 1674, England took over the Dutch territory and made it part of its New York colony.

William Penn received a charter from the King Charles II of England in 1681 to establish Pennsylvania. He soon also took over Delaware, establishing a common representative government for both territories. Delaware was then known as the Three Lower Counties due to its location downriver from Pennsylvania. By 1704, the Three Lower Counties formed their own legislature.

From Colony to State

In the second half of the eighteenth century, many American colonists began to push for independence from England. When the American Revolution broke out in 1775, Delawareans were divided about rebelling. But a number of patriots influenced the colonists to sign the Declaration of Independence on July 2, 1776.

The territory soon penned its first constitution and officially became the state of Delaware. During the Revolutionary War, Delawareans formed one of the most prominent regiments in the Continental Army under George Washington. It was called the Delaware Blues and nicknamed the Blue Hen Chickens (after what later became the official state bird). The British occupied parts of Delaware for a time, and Loyalists (Americans loyal to the British) harassed the revolutionaries in New Castle County.

After the colonies won the Revolutionary War and gained independence from England, colonial statesmen gathered in Philadelphia in 1787 to form a national government. The Constitutional Convention featured prominent Delawareans. On December 7, 1787, Delaware was the first to ratify the Constitution, making it the first state in the Union.

The Nineteenth Century: New Challenges

Delaware faced important changes and challenges in the nineteenth century. The Industrial Revolution was dawning. When the British attacked the United States during the War of 1812, Delaware, cut off from British goods, developed its own industries.

Around this time, Delaware also became an important center for milling flour. Improvements in transportation helped manufacturing

The Fight for Equal Rights in Delaware

The Union's victory in the Civil War in 1865 did not mean that African Americans suddenly enjoyed equal rights. Jim Crow laws segregated Delaware's blacks in housing, education, and public spaces.

Delaware's legislature voted against the Thirteenth, Fourteenth, and Fifteenth amendments to the U.S. Constitution, which, respectively, abolished slavery, guaranteed equal protections for all races, and allowed blacks to vote. It was not until 1901 that Delaware ratified these amendments.

Civil rights–era activism, however, would bring change to Delaware. A school segregation lawsuit was brought by seven parents of African American schoolchildren. They claimed that their children were being forced to attend inferior, run-down, and far distant all-black schools because of their color, despite the existence of good whites-only schools in their neighborhoods. The case was called *Gebhart v. Belton* (1952). It was eventually combined with three other similar lawsuits into the groundbreaking *Brown v. Board of Education* (1954) case that ordered an end to public school segregation throughout the United States. Over time, official segregation in all areas of life was outlawed.

Today, African American Delawareans have entered every profession and attained political influence. Wilmington even elected its first black mayor, James Sills, in 1992.

James Sills, Wilmington's first black mayor, who served from 1993 to 2001.

and trade, linking Delaware to its neighbors and points distant. A canal between Delaware Bay and Chesapeake Bay that opened in 1829 was another important link between Delaware and the other states, allowing it to expand markets for its goods.

In 1838, a railroad connecting Wilmington, Philadelphia, and Baltimore, Maryland, was completed. The advent of steamships and their use on the Delaware River helped Delaware's goods—especially peaches, which the state was known for in the nineteenth century—to reach Northern markets.

A restored version of the Wilmington & Western railroad is now a tourist attraction that preserves the railroad experience of yesteryear.

The Question of Slavery

The Civil War, which divided the United States over the issues of slavery and states' rights, broke out in 1861. At this time, Delaware had as many as twenty thousand freed blacks and fewer than two thousand slaves. Slavery was not nearly as entrenched there as it was in the Southern states. Technically, however, it remained a slave state. Many state legislators tried to change this but repeatedly suffered narrow defeats.

The antislavery movement, known as abolitionism, was strong in Delaware. Blacks and whites alike aided the Underground Railroad, the secret network that helped slaves escape from the South. Delaware's ports and its proximity to free states made it a major "stop" on the railroad.

Delaware became the only slave state not to secede. Though an estimated twelve thousand Delawareans served in Union regiments, a few hundred citizens battled on the Confederate side, mainly in regiments from Maryland and Virginia. However, no official Confederate regiments formed in Delaware. The Union took over Fort Delaware on the Delaware River and used it as a prisoner-of-war camp.

The Postwar Era

The years following the end of World War II were prosperous ones for many Delawareans. While still an industrial and agricultural player, Delaware's service economy in the 1970s greatly expanded. Businesses such as credit card, banking, and financial services soon employed more people than chemical production, for example (for more on Delaware's importance to the chemical industry, see chapter 4).

Because of its business-friendly environment, many companies also incorporated themselves in Delaware. When a company incorporates, or becomes a corporation, it enjoys lower tax rates. It also receives greater protection from lawsuits and debts than do companies that are owned by an individual or run as a partnership. Wilmington went from America's chemical capital to its corporate capital.

Looking to the Future

With its history of business and technological leadership, Delaware continues to change and move forward. For example, CNN reported in July 2008 that Delmarva Power, one of Delaware's main energy

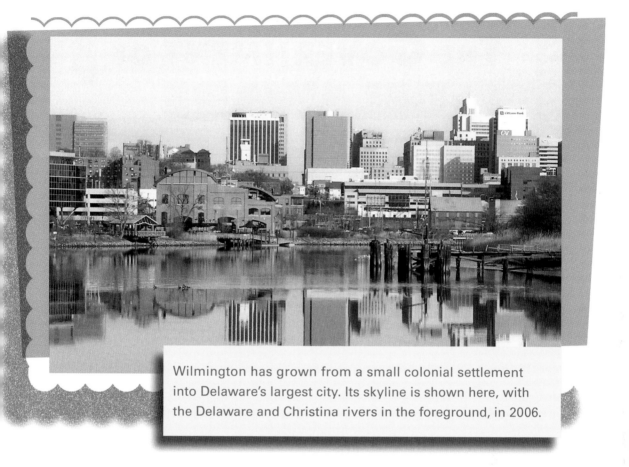

Wilmington has grown from a small colonial settlement into Delaware's largest city. Its skyline is shown here, with the Delaware and Christina rivers in the foreground, in 2006.

companies, had signed an agreement with Bluewater Wind for the nation's first offshore wind farm. It is to be built off the state's Atlantic Coast. It is expected to go online by 2012.

Delaware governor John Markell tells the *News Journal* that the state could become a leader in a nationwide effort to switch from oil and gas to "green" (or environmentally friendly) energy. "Some of the people I've talked to around the country have said that, for this whole idea to really take root, a state—ideally an Eastern state—is going to have to take a leading role," Markell says. With its universities, corporate research centers, and government already working on green technologies, Delaware, for a small state, is thinking big.

Chapter 3

THE GOVERNMENT OF DELAWARE

Delaware's state government is similar to that of many other U.S. states, as well as that of the U.S. federal system. However, Delaware's government retains unique features, some of which date back to colonial times. Its current system is based on the last state constitution, approved in 1897, the fourth in its history.

Delaware's government is divided into three main branches: executive, legislative, and judicial. The legislature passes laws and other measures. The executive branch carries out the laws passed by the state legislature. The judicial branch settles disputes among citizens, government, business, and other parties and decides if laws comply with the state constitution.

The Executive Branch

The executive branch in Delaware is headed by the governor, elected in a popular vote by the people to a four-year term. The governor serves a maximum of two terms, or eight years. The lieutenant governor, similar to a vice president, is also elected for four years. He or she can serve more than two terms, however, and takes over if the governor is removed from office, resigns, or dies in office.

Senate members examine legislation in the Legislative Hall, the Delaware state capitol building in Dover. The Senate, along with the Delaware House, makes up the General Assembly.

Other important elected officials that make up the executive branch include the insurance commissioner, auditor, treasurer, and attorney general, among others. The governor appoints many of the remaining nonelected positions. These include state judges, the secretary of education and the board of education, and members of the executive cabinet.

The Legislative Branch

Delaware's legislature, called the General Assembly, makes the state's laws and regulations. It is bicameral. This means that it is split

Delaware's "Hundreds"

When Delaware's colonial government was formed, it had many features borrowed from the British system of governance. One was dividing counties into smaller units called hundreds, a system that was used in some of Britain's American colonies. In other colonies, a town or township would be the closest equivalent. Historians believe the name may refer to dividing larger regions into groups of one hundred families or ten families of ten members each. It may also have referred to an area of land from which one hundred soldiers could have been drafted to serve the king during wartime.

On October 25, 1682, William Penn ordered Delaware to be divided into hundreds for the purposes of taxation. Each hundred also served as a judicial, legislative, and voting district. The term "hundred" first occurs in records concerning the colony of Delaware in 1687. Originally, there were five hundreds in New Castle County, five in Kent County, and two in Sussex County. As the population grew, several of the hundreds divided, creating new hundreds. By 1875, the total number of hundreds had grown to thirty-three, a number that has remained the same to this day.

A 1964 U.S. Supreme Court case, *Roman v. Sincock*, challenged this system, specifically as it related to state election districts. Times had changed, and the state's population had grown. These growing numbers of citizens were not being adequately represented by the hundreds system, which was based on a much smaller state population. As a result, the hundreds system was changed, and voting districts were redrawn to better reflect the rights of voters. The process of redrawing these districts was referred to as reapportionment.

Today, Delaware is the only state to maintain the hundreds system. The hundreds are primarily useful now for providing geographical points of reference and for assessing property taxes.

into two houses, the state Senate and the state House. It has a total of sixty-two members. The twenty-one state senators serve four-year terms, while the forty-one members of the house (called representatives) serve two-year terms.

The members of the General Assembly are elected from the various towns and areas around the state. Every year, the assembly's legislative session generally lasts from the second Tuesday of January until the end of June. However, the governor or leaders of both houses can call special sessions for important or urgent business.

One unique aspect of Delaware's legislature is its control over state constitutional amendments. It is the only state in which the legislature can approve an amendment to its constitution without the public approving it through a vote.

The Judicial Branch

The state judiciary in Delaware is structured a bit differently than it is in many other states. The highest court is the supreme court, which has the final say on state legal issues. It is comprised of a chief justice and four associate justices appointed for twelve-year terms by the governor, with state senate approval. There is a lower court called the superior court that has branches in each of the three counties.

The Chancery Court

One institution that continues to survive from colonial times is Delaware's chancery court, one of only a handful of such courts that remain throughout the United States. It mainly handles business cases and disputes. These may include lawsuits against the

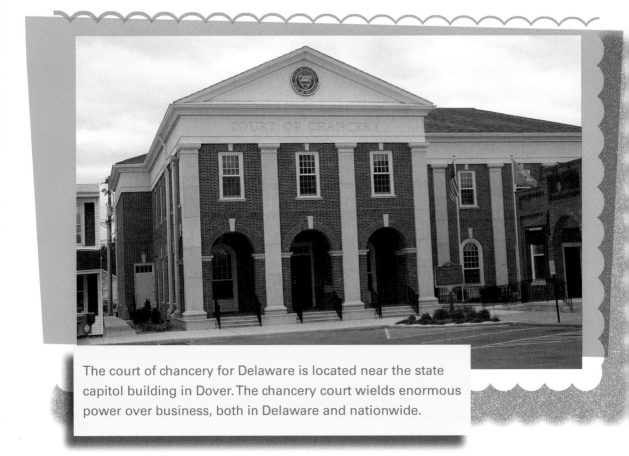

The court of chancery for Delaware is located near the state capitol building in Dover. The chancery court wields enormous power over business, both in Delaware and nationwide.

many companies incorporated in Delaware, corporate mergers and acquisitions, cases brought by employees or consumers, and many other commerce-related legal actions. Chancery judges are also appointed by the governor and approved by the senate for twelve-year terms. The court's jurisdiction also includes certain types of civil rights cases.

Delaware's chancery court has a national impact because its cases often involve national and multinational corporations. The court has traditionally been very business-friendly, with a reputation for efficiency. Its rulings on cases form the basis of Delaware's

General Corporation Law, the statute governing business practices in the state.

County Government

Delaware's three counties each have their own regional governments. New Castle County has an elected president that heads a six-member council. Kent County has an elected county commission, called a levy court, made up of seven members. Sussex County is governed by a five-member council headed by a president. All elected officials in the counties serve four-year terms.

Delaware's state government often handles issues that in larger states might be overseen by county or local governments. These include some legal matters, handled by the state courts, and law enforcement, which is handled by state police.

Delaware and National Politics

Delaware sends only three members to the U.S. Congress. Like all the states, it has two U.S. senators, but only one representative in the U.S. House of Representatives, due to its small population. Because a great deal of funding to the states comes from the U.S. government, Delaware's congressional delegation works hard to ensure that the state gets its fair share of federal dollars. When it comes to U.S. presidential elections, Delaware controls three electoral votes needed for a candidate to win the presidency.

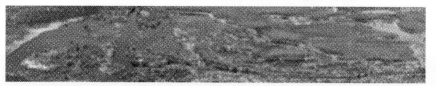

The Economy of Delaware

Chapter 4

Delaware has a diverse economy and leads the nation in many business sectors. If you or your parents own a credit card, you may notice that the return address on the bill envelope bears a Wilmington address. That last chicken meal you had may very well have originated in Delaware's Sussex County. A great many chemicals in your household may have been developed in Delaware, along with the cellophane in your kitchen drawer or nylon in your backpack. It's a good bet that many of the biggest corporations you have heard of are incorporated or headquartered in Delaware.

A Center of Industry

Delaware has been an important center of manufacturing for more than a century. Manufacturing remains one of the pillars of the state's economy, with about 10 percent of its current workforce employed in manufacturing. Chemical production accounts for a large portion of that, most of it in the Wilmington area.

Wilmington's E. I du Pont de Nemours & Co. (or, simply, DuPont) was initially a gunpowder manufacturer. Today, however, it is known as the chemical giant that has developed and marketed thousands of innovative products since the nineteenth century. These include

Thomas Powell, the vice president and general manager of the DuPont company's Advanced Fiber Systems division, holds a spool of Kevlar.

synthetic (or artificial) textiles like Dacron polyester, nylon, rayon, and Lycra spandex; cellophane; Kevlar bulletproof body armor; paints, varnishes, lacquers, and dyes; and even genetically modified (GM) crops. Due to DuPont's leadership in this industry, Wilmington has been called the Chemical Capital of the World. Other leading chemical firms include Atlas and Hercules, Inc.

Delaware produces other manufactured goods, including precision scientific equipment, plastic and rubber products, paper goods, and industrial equipment. The automobile industry also has a sizeable presence in the state. General Motors and Chrysler maintain plants for motor parts and vehicles. Pharmaceuticals (prescription and

Delaware's Economy

As in many U.S. states, Delaware's economy has changed greatly since colonial times. From its agricultural beginnings, the state grew as a manufacturing center in the eighteenth and nineteenth centuries. In Wilmington and elsewhere, earlier immigrants flocked to jobs in the steamboat, railroad car, carriage, and leather goods manufacturing industries. By the first half of the twentieth century, Delaware workers were making chemicals and other innovative products, like plastics and synthetic textiles (fabrics), for companies such as DuPont.

But the latter half of the twentieth century brought great changes. The 1970s were a time of industrial decline in the United States. Delaware, feeling the pinch of economic slowdown, passed laws to attract banks, especially their credit card divisions. Many of these laws allowed credit card companies to make more money on their services and pay lower taxes than they would elsewhere in the country.

While industry remains an important part of Delaware's economy, many manufacturing jobs have been replaced by positions in the service sector. Banking, credit card processing, insurance, real estate, and professional services grew rapidly in the last three decades. They now account for an estimated 86 percent of Delaware's workforce, according to the U.S. Department of Labor. A quick look at Delaware's employment statistics reveals how diverse (varied) the state's economy is. The state's leading industries, in terms of the number of people employed by them, are (in descending order):

- Trade, transportation, and utilities
- Government
- Education and health services
- Professional and business services
- Financial activities
- Leisure, hospitality, and tourism
- Manufacturing
- Mining, logging, and construction

over-the-counter drugs) are also big business in Delaware, especially in the Wilmington area.

Banking, Incorporation, and Services

Delaware is considered a capital of corporate America because of its unique tax policies and incorporation law. While the business-friendly incorporation law was passed in 1899, it wasn't until the second half of the twentieth century that thousands of major corporations began incorporating in the state. According to Delaware.gov, these currently include more than half of all publicly traded corporations in the United States, as well as 63 percent of all Fortune 500 companies (the list of the largest five hundred U.S. firms).

It is estimated that as many as 850,000 companies and businesses incorporate in Delaware. The great majority of these companies actually have a minimal presence in the state. In fact, their headquarters and main branches are usually elsewhere. Companies pay a yearly $50 fee to incorporate, with this income accounting for about 20 percent of Delaware's annual state budget.

Delaware's business-friendly environment extends to the banking and financial services industries, as well. A law passed in 1981, the Financial Center Development Act, paved the way for Delaware to become a center of banking, especially credit card operations. Other service industries, including legal and insurance services, took hold in Delaware because of the banking sector's rise.

Agriculture

Agriculture is another pillar of Delaware's economy with most of the state's activity centered in southern Sussex County. The United

Chickens belonging to Sussex County farmer William Brook are pictured here in April 2006, two weeks before reaching market size.

States Department of Agriculture (USDA) estimates that Delaware has about 2,200 farms, a majority of them owned by small operators.

Raising and processing poultry is the major economic activity in southern Delaware. The state's main farm product is broilers, which are five- to twelve-week-old chickens. Besides broilers and other poultry, Delaware produces a diverse array of farm products. Soybeans account for about 40 percent of the state's cultivated land. Corn is also raised, mainly to feed livestock. Other crops include wheat, peaches, apples, nuts, berries, melons, and potatoes, mainly for local markets. Farmers also raise pigs and dairy cows. According to the USDA, approximately 79 percent of Delaware's agricultural income in 2007 came from livestock and related products, while crops accounted for about 21 percent.

Tourism

Every year, thousands of tourists and vacationers visit Delaware. Hikers enjoy the scenic countryside of northern Delaware's Piedmont region. Dover and other cities are full of well-preserved colonial attractions, including centuries-old churches, courthouses, meeting halls, forts, homesteads, and houses. Visitors come for the history, and many enjoy the added bonus of tax-free shopping.

Delaware's Atlantic Coast beaches help drive its economy. For day-trippers and summer residents, destinations include Bethany, Fenwick Island, and Lewes. The most popular, Rehoboth

A sand castle constructed on Rehoboth Beach, perhaps Delaware's most popular summertime destination.

Beach, calls itself the Nation's Summer Capital because of its many visitors from the Washington, D.C., area.

The Public Sector

One of Delaware's largest employers is Delaware itself—in other words, the public, or government, sector. Because it is small in size and population, a somewhat larger percentage of its people work for the government than in other states. Many government jobs are naturally located in and around Dover, the state capital. Public sector employment is composed of local, state, and federal level jobs. These include positions in the courts, schools, postal service, government offices, public utilities (such as power plants), museums, state parks, and the highway department.

Chapter 5

PEOPLE FROM DELAWARE:
PAST AND PRESENT

Delaware's progress from colonial times to the present is closely linked to unique individuals who have made a difference in the state. Colonial-era patriots, industrialists, politicians, African American leaders, philanthropists, and many others have all contributed greatly to Delaware's story.

John Dickinson, "Penman of the Revolution"

John Dickinson, born in 1732, studied law and was prominent in both Delaware and Pennsylvania. He became famous for writing newspaper articles against British taxation of the colonies. These were later reprinted as a pamphlet, "Letters from a Farmer in Pennsylvania to the Inhabitants of the British Colonies." These writings inspired the anti-British cause, earning Dickinson the nickname Penman of the Revolution.

Interestingly, when Dickinson participated in the Continental Congress, he opposed the Declaration of Independence. But he served loyally in the Continental Army. He later helped to write the Articles of Confederation, the governing document that preceded the U.S. Constitution.

32

A relief engraved by artist James Edward Kelly (1855–1933) depicts Delaware patriot Caesar Rodney's crucial and famous vote for liberty in Independence Hall on July 4, 1776.

Caesar Rodney: Riding for Independence

Another Delaware patriot, Caesar Rodney, was born in 1728 into a wealthy and influential Kent County farm family. He rose from the position of sheriff of Kent County to other political posts. By the 1760s, he began to push for independence from the British.

Rodney was a delegate to the Stamp Act Congress of 1765, held to oppose unfair British taxation. In June 1775, Rodney was speaker of the assembly of the lower counties when the assembly voted to split from the British. War broke out, and Rodney became a brigadier general in Delaware's militia, in which he had earlier served. Rodney

The du Ponts

Eleuthère Irénée du Pont (1771-1834) was a French entrepreneur who settled in Delaware in 1800. Du Pont started a gunpowder business on the Brandywine River in 1802. Du Pont eventually made huge profits supplying the U.S. military. In fact, du Pont supplied about half of all the gunpowder used by the Union Army during the Civil War.

A portrait of E. I. du Pont.

At the beginning of the twentieth century, Pierre du Pont, E. I. du Pont's great-grandson, expanded DuPont into a multinational chemical corporation. Over the years, the company created and sold groundbreaking products that became everyday household items. These included:

- Dacron (polyester)
- Lucite (a plastic alternative to glass)
- Kevlar (used in bulletproof vests and body armor, among other things)

- Teflon (a nonstick cooking surface)
- Lycra (an elastic synthetic fiber often used in activewear)
- Paints, dyes, insecticides, and refrigerants

Some du Ponts helped run the business, while others became politicians. Many were philanthropists, donating money to build schools, museums, and highways. Numerous landmarks and institutions bear their name to this day.

No du Pont has run the family business since 1971, though many heirs still hold company stock. Perhaps the most prominent du Pont of recent years is Pete du Pont, a three-term Delaware congressman and governor from 1977 to 1985. As governor, he is credited with reviving the state's economy by attracting credit card companies. He now works as a lawyer, newspaper columnist, and policy analyst."

is perhaps most famous, however, for his heroic ride to the Continental Congress of 1776. This enabled Delaware's delegation to cast its vote in favor of the Declaration of Independence.

Emily Bissell: Christmas Seals Pioneer

In 1907, an American Red Cross member and fund-raiser named Emily Bissell was asked by her cousin Dr. Joseph Wales to raise money for Brandywine Sanatorium, a place of recovery for tuberculosis (TB) patients.

Inspired by a similar charity campaign in Denmark, she decided to sell decorative seals to be placed on postage envelopes sent during the Christmas holidays. Borrowing money from friends, she designed and printed fifty thousand seals. She initially sold them at a Wilmington post office for one cent each, allowing even people of modest means to help fight TB.

Once Bissell publicized her campaign, news stories appeared nationwide about her cause. Over the last century, Christmas Seals have raised millions of dollars annually to fight lung diseases. A public hospital outside Wilmington was even named in Bissell's honor.

James M. Baker: From Riots to Rebirth

When civil rights leader Martin Luther King Jr. was assassinated in 1968, Wilmington was one of many American cities where black citizens' grief and anger boiled over into riots. At the time, a community service volunteer named James M. Baker was working with both youth groups and gang members as part of a federal antipoverty program. A week of rioting led to the city being occupied by the National Guard for more than nine months.

Baker's experiences inspired him to fight for fairness and black economic empowerment. He eventually rose to the position of district councilman and, later, Wilmington's first black city council president in 1985. In 2001, Baker became the city's mayor. In January 2009, Baker was again reelected, making him the city's first mayor ever elected to three terms.

Joseph Biden Jr.: Favorite Son

Perhaps no Delawarean has been as prominent in national politics over the last few decades as Joseph Biden Jr. Capping an extraordinary political career, he was inaugurated in January 2009 as vice president under President Barack Obama. Hailing from a blue-collar background, Biden attended the University of Delaware. He later became a lawyer and member of the New Castle County council. In 1972, the twenty-nine-year-old Biden was one of the youngest people elected to the U.S. Senate. He would serve six terms there representing Delaware.

Biden became a prominent senator, known for major anticrime and domestic violence legislation, and eventually served as longtime chairman of the Foreign Relations Committee. He has also secured federal dollars for Delaware. These included the building of a modern poultry disease facility at the University of Delaware, helping expand the state police, preserving Delaware's coastline, and providing health care for children.

From a humble background on to decades of Senate service and finally the White House, Biden has always stayed true to his Delaware roots. Instead of moving to Washington, D.C., Biden commuted to the Senate for years so he could remain with his family in Wilmington. As longtime friend John Martilla tells the *Los Angeles Times*, "You get to know Joe Biden the closer you get to Wilmington."

His years of Senate experience have helped U.S. vice president Joe Biden become an important player on the Obama team.

Jack Markell, Governor

In January 2009, Democrat Jack Markell became the seventy-third governor of Delaware. The ceremony took place at the University of Delaware, his alma mater. It was also a historic moment, since Markell is the state's first Jewish governor.

Born and bred in Newark, Markell held several executive jobs in corporate America. He won praise during three terms as state treasurer for tightening the budget and innovative health programs for state workers.

Timeline

1609	Henry Hudson explores the Delaware Bay and Delaware River.
1610	Captain Samuel Argall gives Delaware Bay its name.
1638	Fort Christina is founded by Swedes at the site of present-day Wilmington.
1681	William Penn receives a charter that gives him control of Pennsylvania and Delaware.
1704	Known as the Three Lower Counties, Delaware sets up its first independent legislature.
1775	American colonists start the Revolutionary War against England.
1776	After Caesar Rodney's ride to sign the Declaration of Independence, Delaware officially revolts against England.
1787	On December 7, Delaware becomes the first state in the Union by being the first to ratify the U.S. Constitution.
1861–1865	Thousands of Delawareans fight in the Civil War, most on the Union side.
1880	Rehoboth Beach holds the "Miss United States" beauty pageant, thought to be the first one in the United States.
1897	Delaware adopts its fourth, and final, state constitution.
1899	The state passes the Delaware Corporation Law.
1907	The state's first automobile is licensed in Delaware. Emily Bissell pioneers the use of Christmas Seals in the United States to fight tuberculosis.
1968	Riots following the assassination of Martin Luther King Jr. erupt in Wilmington, prompting a months-long occupation of the city by the National Guard.
1971	Delaware passes the Delaware Coastal Zone Act, moving to protect its coastal areas from industrial development.
1981	The Financial Center Development Act is passed to attract banks to Delaware.
1992	James Sills is elected the first black mayor of Wilmington.
2001	Ruth Ann Minner is elected Delaware's first female governor.
2009	Jack Markell is inaugurated as Delaware's first Jewish governor.

State motto	"Liberty and Independence"
State capital	Dover
State bird	Blue hen chicken
State tree	American holly
State flower	Peach blossom
Statehood date and number	December 7, 1787; the first state
State nickname	The First State; the Blue Hen State; the Diamond State; the Small Wonder
Total area and U.S. rank	1,982 square miles (5,133 sq km); forty-ninth largest state
Population	783,600; estimated population in 2010: 896,880
Length of coastline	260 miles (418 km)
Highest elevation	Ebright Azimuth, 447.85 feet (136.5 m) above sea level
Lowest elevation	Sea level along the coast

State Flag

State Seal

Major rivers	The Mispillion, St. Jones, Leipsic, Broadkill, Delaware, Nanticoke, and Smyrna rivers. The Christina River and Brandywine Creek are tributaries of the Delaware River.
Major lakes	None
Hottest temperature recorded	110°F (43°C) at Millsboro, on July 21, 1930,
Coldest temperature recorded	-17°F (-27°C) at Millsboro, on January 17, 1893
Origin of state name	Delaware was named to honor the early Virginia governor, Lord De La Warr
Chief agricultural products	Poultry (broilers), soybeans, corn, wheat, potatoes, peaches, melons
Major industries	Trade, transportation, and utilities; government; education and health services; professional and business services; financial activities; leisure, hospitality, and tourism; manufacturing (including chemicals); mining, logging, construction

Blue hen chicken

Peach blossom

abolitionism The movement to end slavery in the United States prior to the Civil War.

arc A part or section of a circle.

bicameral Refers to a legislature made up of two separate representative voting bodies.

broiler A chicken five to twelve weeks old; one of Delaware's most important products.

entrepreneur A person who starts a privately owned business.

executive The branch of government that carries out, or executes, its laws.

Fortune 500 The list of the five hundred largest manufacturing companies in the world, as determined by *Fortune* magazine.

hundreds A colonial-era system of land division in Delaware's counties; each hundred (a unit of land area) formed a voting district and was subject to a certain rate of property tax.

judiciary The branch of government that handles legal disputes and judges whether laws are constitutional.

legislative The branch of government that writes and passes laws.

Lenape A Native American people who lived in Delaware and throughout the Mid-Atlantic states before European settlement.

Loyalist A person loyal to the British during the Revolutionary War.

mean A numerical average measurement, as in mean temperature.

philanthropist A wealthy person who donates money to worthy causes, such as the arts, education, antipoverty programs, third world development, or health care and medical research.

public sector Refers to those employed by the local, state, or federal government.

synthetic Refers to artificially created materials, including fabrics or other products.

tuberculosis An infectious disease that affects the human respiratory system.

Underground Railroad A secret network of individuals that banded together to help escaped slaves from the South reach freedom in the North.

Delaware Department of Agriculture

2320 South DuPont Highway

Dover, DE 19901

(302) 698-4500

Web site: http://dda.delaware.gov

The Delaware Department of Agriculture's Web site provides statistics, reports, and other information about the state's agricultural output and industry.

Delaware Historical Society

505 North Market Street

Wilmington, DE 19801

(302) 655-7161

Web site: http://www.hsd.org

The Delaware Historical Society is a nonprofit organization that promotes and preserves Delaware's history and heritage.

Delaware Museum of Natural History

4840 Kennett Pike

P.O. Box 3937

Wilmington, DE 19807

(302) 658-9111

Web site: http://www.delmnh.org

The museum aims to educate citizens on Delaware's indigenous species and resources.

Delaware Public Archives

121 Duke of York Street

Dover, DE 19901

Web site: http://archives.delaware.gov/default.shtml

The home page for Delaware's public archives features links to historical accounts, pictures, audio, and other media.

Hagley Museum and Library

200 Hagley Road

Wilmington, DE 19807

(302) 658-2400

Web site: http://www.hagley.lib.de.us

The Hagley Museum and Library collects, preserves, and exhibits artifacts and other materials relating to Delaware's and the United States' industrial history.

State of Delaware Division of Historical and Cultural Affairs

21 The Green

Dover, DE 19901

(302) 736-7400

Web site: http://history.delaware.org

The official state agency handles the preservation of history and heritage in Delaware.

Web Sites

Due to the changing nature of Internet links, Rosen Publishing has developed an online list of Web sites related to the subject of this book. This site is updated regularly. Please use this link to access this list:

http://www.rosenlinks.com/uspp/depp

FOR FURTHER READING

Blashfield, Jean F. *The Delaware Colony* (Spirit of America—Our Colonies). Mankato, MN: Child's World, 2003.

Brown, Jonatha A. *Delaware* (Portraits of the States). Strongsville, OH: Gareth Stevens Publishing, 2006.

Doherty, Craig A., and Katherine M. Doherty. *Delaware* (Thirteen Colonies). New York, NY: Facts on File, 2005.

Dubois, Muriel L. *The Delaware Colony* (Fact Finders: The American Colonies). Bloomington, MN: Capstone Press, 2006.

Heinrichs, Ann. *Delaware* (America the Beautiful). Danbury, CT: Children's Press, 2009.

Marsh, Carole. *Delaware Native Americans* (Carole Marsh State Books). Peachtree City, GA: Gallopade, 2004.

Miller, Amy. *Delaware* (From Sea to Shining Sea). Danbury, CT: Children's Press, 2009.

Raymond, Aaron. *A Primary Source History of the Colony of Delaware* (13 Colonies). New York, NY: Rosen Publishing, 2006.

Reiter, Chris. *Delaware* (States). Berkeley Heights, NJ: Enslow Publishers, 2003.

Rendle, Ellen. *Historic Photos of Delaware*. Nashville, TN: Turner Publishing Co., 2008.

Rubin, Beth. *Delaware Curiosities: Quirky Characters, Roadside Oddities, and Other Offbeat Stuff*. Guilford, CT: Globe Pequot Press, 2007.

Weslager, C. A. *Delaware's Forgotten Folk: The Story of the Moors and Nanticokes*. Philadelphia, PA: University of Pennsylvania Press, 2006.

Wimmer, Teresa. *Delaware* (This Land Called America). Mankato, MN: Creative Education, 2008.

Worth, Richard. *Delaware* (Life in the Thirteen Colonies). Danbury, CT: Children's Press, 2004.

BIBLIOGRAPHY

Boyd, Gerald M. "The Paradox of Pete du Pont: Political Iconoclast with Establishment Roots." *New York Times*, December 28, 1987. Section A, p. 18.

Brozyna, Christine. "Get to Know Joe Biden." ABC News, December 13, 2007. Retrieved February 2009 (http://abcnews.go.com/WN/WhoIs/story?id=3770445&page=1).

Chase, Randall. "Tiny Delaware Big on History." Associated Press, July 19, 2003. Retrieved February 2009 (http://fredericksburg.com/News/FLS/2003/072003/0719 2003/1036591/index_html).

City of Wilmington home page. "The City of Wilmington." Retrieved February 2009 (http://www.ci.wilmington.de.us/history.htm).

Courson, Paul. "Wind Farm to Be Built off Delaware Shore." CNN, June 23, 2008. Retrieved February 2009 (http://www.cnn.com/2008/TECH/06/23/wind.turbines/index.html).

Delaware.gov. "Biography of Delaware Governor John Markell." Retrieved February 2009 (http://governor.delaware.gov/biography.shtml).

Delaware.gov. "Delaware Facts and Symbols." Retrieved February 2009 (http://portal.delaware.gov/delfacts/default.shtml).

Delaware.gov. "The Hundreds of Delaware." Retrieved February 2009 (http://history.delaware.gov/museums/vc/vc_hundreds.shtml).

Fontes, Justine, and Ron Fontes. *The First State* (World Almanac Library of the States). Strongsville, OH: Gareth Stevens Publishing, 2003.

Levey, Noam M. "In His Home State, Biden Is a Regular Joe." TruthOut, August 24, 2008 (http://www.truthout.org/article/in-his-home-state-biden-a-regular-joe).

Miller, Beth. "Markell Takes Oath as Delaware's 73rd Governor." *News Journal*, January 19, 2009. Retrieved February 2009 (http://www.delawareonline.com/article/20090119/NEWS/901 20001).

Moncure, Sue. "Book Examines Delaware Patriot's Life and Times." University of Delaware, August 24, 2000. Retrieved February 2009 (http://www.udel.edu/PR/UpDate/00/38/caesar.html).

Montgomery, Jeff. "Markell Looks to 'Green Is Gold' Future." *News Journal*, February 15, 2009. Retrieved February 2009 (http://www.delmarvanow.com/article/20090215/NEWS01/90215003/1002/rss).

Moose, Katie. *Uniquely Delaware* (Heinemann State Studies). Portsmouth, NH: Heinemann Library, 2003.

Munroe, John A. *History of Delaware*. Newark, DE: University of Delaware Press, 2006.

Parsons, Donald F., Jr., and Joseph R. Sights III. "The History of Delaware's Business Courts." American Bar Association, March 3, 2008. Retrieved February 2009 (http://www.abanet.org/buslaw/blt/2008-03-04/slights.shtml).

Taylor, Adam. "Wilmington Riots: 40 Years Later: Many See Riots as Necessary Evil That Set in Motion Racial Progress." *News Journal*, April 6, 2008. Retrieved February 2009 (http://www.delawareonline.com/apps/pbcs.dll/article?AID=/20080406/NEWS02/804060349).

Time. "The Wizards of Wilmington." April 16, 1951. Retrieved February 2009 (http://www.time.com/time/magazine/article/0,9171,814737-1,00.html).

U.S. Census Bureau. "2000 Census Data for Delaware." Retrieved February 2009 (http://www.census.gov/census2000/states/de.html).

U.S. Department of Agriculture. "Delaware Fact Sheet." 2007. Retrieved February 2009 (http://www.ers.usda.gov/StateFacts/DE.htm#TCEC).

U.S. Department of Labor, Bureau of Labor Statistics (BLS). "Delaware." 2008. Retrieved February 2009 (http://www.bls.gov/ro3/ro3_de.htm).

U.S. Geological Survey. "Science in Your Backyard: Delaware." Retrieved February 2009 (http://www.usgs.gov/state/state.asp?State=DE).

Weslager, C. A. *The Delaware Indians*. New Brunswick, NJ: Rutgers University Press, 1990.

INDEX

About the Author

Philip Wolny is a writer and editor raised in New York. During his fairly extensive U.S. travels, he has visited many states. In his experience, however, few have offered the combination of hospitality and history that he experienced in Delaware a few years back. The research Wolny did for this book has inspired him to plan a return visit to the First State.

Photo Credits

Designer: Les Kanturek; Photo Researcher: Marty Levick